Grammar, Reading & Maths 10-Minute Tests Ages 8–9

T0371168

10-Minute Tests

KS2 Year 4

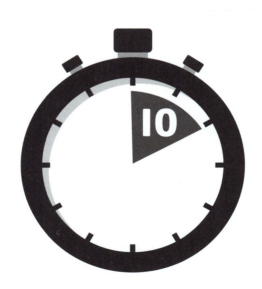

Track progress with 10-minute skills checks

Published in the UK by Scholastic, 2019

Scholastic Distribution Centre, Bosworth Avenue, Tournament Fields, Warwick, CV34 6UQ

Scholastic Ireland, 89E Lagan Road, Dublin Industrial Estate, Glasnevin, Dublin, D11 HP5F

SCHOLASTIC and associated logos are trademarks and/or registered trademarks of Scholastic Inc.

www.scholastic.co.uk

4 5 6 7 8 9   4 5 6 7 8 9 0 1 2 3

A CIP catalogue record for this book is available from the British Library.
ISBN 978-1407-18315-2

Printed and bound by Bell & Bain, Glasgow, UK.

The book is made of materials from well-managed, FSC®-certified forests and other controlled sources.

MIX
Paper | Supporting
responsible forestry
FSC® C007785

Authors
Grammar, Punctuation and Spelling: Shelley Welsh

Reading: Giles Clare

Maths: Paul Hollin

Editorial Rachel Morgan, Vicki Yates, Kate Pedlar, Kate Baxter, Suzanne Adams, Gemma Smith

Design Nicolle Thomas and Neil Salt, Dan Prescott/Couper Street Type Co and Jayne Rawlings/Oxford Raw Design

Cover Illustration Tania Bondar

Illustration Karen Donnelly/D'Avila Illustration

Technical artwork Darren Lingard/D'Avila Illustration

Acknowledgements
The publishers gratefully acknowledge permission to reproduce the following copyright material: Macmillan Children's Books for the use of the 'The Fox and the Grapes' by Celia Warren from The Works chosen by Paul Cookson. Text © Celia Warren. (Pan Macmillan, 2010).

Photograph
page 25: tiger, Dmitriy Kochergin/Shutterstock

Contents

10 MINS

How to use this book

10 MINS

This book contains three grammar, punctuation and spelling tests, three reading tests and two sets of maths tests for Year 4. The tests provide a wide coverage of the national curriculum for this age group.

Grammar, punctuation and spelling

It is intended that children will take around ten minutes to complete each test. Each test is in two parts and comprises 11 or 12 grammar and punctuation questions and four spelling questions. For example, Grammar and Punctuation Test 1 and Spelling Test 1 make up one full test which should take ten minutes to complete.

Grammar and punctuation tests

Each test comprises 11 or 12 questions, which amount to 12 marks in total. Some questions require a selected response, where children select the correct answer from a list. Other questions require a constructed response, where children insert a word or punctuation mark, or write a short answer of their own.

Spelling tests

There are four questions in each test, amounting to four marks. Read each spelling number followed by *The word is...* Read the context sentence and then repeat *The word is...* Leave at least a 12-second gap between spellings. More information can be found on page 61.

Reading

Each test comprises a text followed by comprehension questions. There is one fiction, one non-fiction and one poetry text. It is intended that children will take approximately ten minutes to complete each test. Some questions require a selected response, where children choose the correct answer from several options. Other questions require a constructed response, where children write a short or extended answer of their own.

Maths

It is intended that children will take approximately ten minutes to complete each individual test; or approximately 30 minutes to complete each set of three tests. Some questions require a selected response, for example where children choose the correct answer from several options. Other questions require a constructed response, where children work out and write down their own answer.

Marking the tests

A mark scheme and a progress chart are also included towards the end of this book. After your child has completed a test, mark it and together identify and practise any areas where your child is less confident. Ask them to complete the next test at a later date, when you feel they have had enough time to practise and improve.

Grammar and Punctuation
Test 1

Marks

1. Underline the **two nouns** in the sentence below.

I put my book on the shelf.

1

---

2. Which sentence below is **punctuated** correctly?

Tick **one**.

Why don't we go swimming tomorrow! ☐

What a brilliant idea that is! ☐

Let's ask Dad if he'll take us? ☐

How excited I am? ☐

1

---

3. Draw a line to match each word to the correct **prefix** to make the opposite meaning.

im	available
un	agree
dis	possible

1

KEEP IT GOING!

Marks

4. Tick one box in each row to show whether the underlined words in each sentence are a **main clause** or a **subordinate clause**.

Sentence	Main clause	Subordinate clause
I packed my waterproofs <u>because it might rain later</u>.		
<u>Mum likes singing</u> even though she can't sing a note!		
<u>After we had mixed the solution</u>, we left it near the heater so that the water would evaporate.		

1

5. Insert **two commas** in the correct places in the sentence below.

My dog likes going for walks fetching sticks swimming and chasing rabbits.

1

6. Change the adjectives below into **adverbs** by adding the **suffix** 'ly'. You may need to remove or change a letter.

mad   _____

special   _____

angry   _____

1

Marks

7. Draw a line to match each pair of words on the left to its correct **contraction**.

we'd

we had

we've

we are

wev'e

we have

we'ad

we're

1

8. Replace the underlined words in the sentence below with a **pronoun**.

Mum opened the door and then closed <u>the door</u> with a bang.

1

9. Circle the words in the sentence below which should start with a **capital letter**.

we went to london on the bus and visited buckingham palace.

1

10 MINS

Marks

10. Which **verb form** completes the sentence below?

After they _____ their homework, Cathy and Stefan watched a film.

Tick **one**.

were finishing ☐

have finished ☐

are finished ☐

had finished ☐

1

11. Circle the **possessive pronoun** in the sentence below.

I tried Claire's homemade chocolate brownies and then she tried mine.

1

12. Which sentence below is an **exclamation**?

Tick **one**.

What an amazing book that was ☐

You've read it, haven't you ☐

I must lend it to Sami ☐

Do you know if there's a sequel ☐

1

Well done! END OF GRAMMAR & PUNCTUATION TEST 1!

Grammar and Punctuation
Test 2

10 MINS

1. Underline the **adverb** in the sentence below.

The children walked quietly into the assembly hall.

1

2. Tick the sentence below that is a **statement**.

Tick **one**.

What a nuisance my little brother can be! ☐

I have two sisters and one brother. ☐

Do you have any brothers or sisters? ☐

Tell me their names. ☐

1

3. Draw a line to match each word to the correct **prefix** on the left to make the opposite meaning.

un   appear

dis   helpful

mis   spell

1

10 MINS

Marks

4. Circle the two **determiners** in the sentence below.

Dan leaned against a tree while he waited for the bus.

1

5. Complete the sentence below with **two** different **co-ordinating conjunctions**.

Mia _____ Ed really enjoyed the film _____ Ushma found it boring.

1

6. Which **verb form** completes the sentence so that it shows a continuous action in the past?

As they _____ the performance, the fire alarm went off.

Tick **one**.

watch ☐

are watching ☐

were watching ☐

had watched ☐

1

Marks

7. What is the **word class** of the underlined word in the sentence below?

Amie kicked the ball <u>over</u> the hedge.

Tick **one**.

pronoun ☐

conjunction ☐

determiner ☐

preposition ☐

1

8. Insert the missing **inverted commas** in the direct speech below.

Let's decide what to buy Mum for her birthday, Martha said to Dad.

1

9. Write the **plural form** of each word below.

box   _____

class   _____

child   _____

1

KEEP IT GOING!

Marks

10. a. Circle the word in the sentence below that uses an **apostrophe** to show **missing letters**.

It's been ages since Mum's sister has visited us.

1

b. Circle the word in the sentence below that uses an **apostrophe** to show **possession**.

I haven't seen Faye's new dog, have you?

1

11. Tick one box in each row to show whether the underlined words are a **main clause** or a **subordinate clause**.

Sentence	Main clause	Subordinate clause
I sheltered under a huge tree <u>because it was raining</u>.		
When we had finished practising our times tables, <u>our teacher tested us</u>.		
<u>We brought our waterproofs on the picnic</u> even though it was a sunny day.		

1

Well done! END OF GRAMMAR & PUNCTUATION TEST 2!

Grammar and Punctuation
Test 3

10 MINS

Marks

1. Underline the **adjective** in the sentence below.

What an enormous spider there is in our bathroom!

1

2. Which sentence below is a **command**?

Tick **one**.

You really must wash your hands before eating ☐

Have you washed your hands yet ☐

Wash your hands before eating ☐

It's important to wash your hands before eating ☐

1

3. Insert the missing **apostrophe** in the sentence below.

Graces books turned up in the lost property box.

1

4. Insert a suitable **subordinating conjunction** in the sentence below.

The doctor prescribed some tablets for me

_____ I had an infection.

1

14

Marks

5. Add the **suffix** 'ly' to each adjective below to form an **adverb**. Write each new word on the line.

regular _____

happy _____

final _____

1

6. Which sentence below is written using correct **grammar**?

Tick **one**.

My brother done his homework while watching TV.

He should of done it in his bedroom. ☐

Mum's always saying we need peace and quiet. ☐

But my brother doesn't listen no more. ☐

1

7. Insert the **two** missing **commas** in the sentence below.

Dougie gave me a hat a pair of slippers a scarf and some socks for my birthday.

1

KEEP IT GOING!

10 MINS

Marks

8. Which sentence is **punctuated** correctly?

Tick **one**.

After, our picnic, we lay in the sun and dozed. ☐

After our picnic we lay, in the sun and dozed. ☐

After our picnic we lay in the sun, and dozed. ☐

After our picnic, we lay in the sun and dozed. ☐

1

9. Which sentence uses the **verb** <u>perform</u> to show a continuous action in the present?

Tick **one**.

We were performing a gymnastics routine for our parents. ☐

We performed a gymnastics routine for our parents. ☐

We are performing a gymnastics routine for our parents. ☐

We have been performing a gymnastics routine for our parents. ☐

1

10. Circle the word that is a **possessive pronoun** in the sentence below.

I shared my sandwiches with Jill yesterday, so today she's sharing hers.

1

Marks

11. Tick **one** box in each row to show if the sentence is in the **present** or the **past tense**.

Sentence	Present tense	Past tense
There are 28 pupils in my class this year.		
Mum and I went to the farm to get some eggs.		
Our neighbours had a leak in their bathroom.		

1

12. Which sentence must end with an **exclamation mark**?

Tick **one**.

What an amazing time we had at the cinema

The new Harry Potter film is so exciting ☐

Have you been to see it yet ☐

Go soon before it's too late ☐

1

Spelling Tests 1 & 2

Spelling Test 1

1. Beth started _____ when she cut her finger.

2. The _____ was frozen after a frosty night.

3. I dressed up as a _____ for Halloween.

4. Our puppy always _____ us.

4

Well done! END OF SPELLING TEST 1!

Spelling Test 2

Marks

1. We are learning about evaporation in _____ .

2. I showed Mum _____ she had left her bag.

3. The football pitch was in a poor _____ .

4. Jon had a good _____ for learning his tables.

4

Well done! END OF SPELLING TEST 2!

Spelling Test 3

Spelling Test 3

Marks

1. I _____ the sugar and flour, then added the butter.

2. We heard an _____ at the back of the cave.

3. The _____ bowed as the audience clapped.

4. Everyone _____ Bhavini could dive off the board.

4

Well done! END OF SPELLING TEST 3!

The Trip

As I entered the playground, the four of them were talking animatedly in a huddle. Eloise, jabbing a finger at Nicola, seemed to be issuing orders again. As I tried to pass them, I saw Jamal flash a look at the others and whisper something urgently. Henry glanced in my direction, his face twisting into a sneer. Next to him, Nicola dropped her head, but I could still see the colour surging to her cheeks through her hair.

A feeling of dread rose in my chest. What were they planning this time? I had only been at my new school for two weeks, but it already felt like forever. "Why do you speak funny?" Eloise had asked the first breaktime. And then at lunch: "Why did you come to our school? Why don't you go back where you came from? Who gave you permission to look at me?" Jamal and Henry had jeered and agreed. Nicola, always standing just behind the others, had giggled but wouldn't meet my gaze. From then on, I had tried my best to avoid them, but they had soon come looking for me.

I half-walked, half-jogged to the end of the playground by the field. A voice called out, "Oi, Thandie, wanna play?" Reluctantly, I glanced over my shoulder. Eloise – flanked by Jamal and Henry, with Nicola behind – was smiling sweetly. I shook my head. "Come on," Eloise said. "We're playing tag."

"No. I mean, no fanks," I said.

Eloise grinned coldly. "No fanks! No *fffanks*." She took a quick step towards me and I flinched. "Poor freaky Fffandie can't even say her own name right, can you? Is it 'cos you're a bit fffick, Fffandie?"

"I'm not… I'm not fthfick," I protested, but my throat was dry and I cursed my voice for cracking. I backed away another step and heard my shoes squelch on muddy grass.

Eloise stole a look back up the playground. "It's okay, coast's clear," confirmed Jamal. "We'll watch for Mrs Slade."

Eloise narrowed her eyes. "You ready for tag, Fffandie? You'd better run – cos I'm it!" She took a purposeful stride towards me. Icy fear crackled through my body and froze my arms and legs. I stared in horror at Eloise. Out of the corner of my eye, I glimpsed movement. A foot. A foot stuck out. A foot that caught Eloise's leg from behind. As Eloise tripped, it was enough to break the spell. I stumbled backwards as Eloise slapped face first into the muddy ground. Jamal and Henry spun round, dumbfounded. Nicola bent over to help the spluttering girl to her feet. Eloise's eyes burned with outrage and embarrassment in her mud-caked face.

"What happened?" asked Jamal.

"I dunno. She just fell," replied Nicola, who glanced up and winked at me.

1. Look at the first sentence. Which of these words is closest in meaning to the word <u>animatedly</u>?

Tick **one**.

casually ☐

quietly ☐

eagerly ☐

carefully ☐

Marks

1

Marks

2. How do we know that Eloise is the leader of the group of children?

_____

_____

1

3. Why does Thandie say it feels like she has been at her new school forever?

_____

_____

_____

_____

2

4. a. What game does Eloise say the children are going to play?

_____

1

b. Who watched out for Mrs Slade?

_____

1

KEEP IT GOING!

Marks

5. *Eloise stole a look back up the playground.*

Why does she do this?

_____

_____

1

6. Read the paragraph beginning: *Eloise narrowed her eyes.*
Find and **copy** the word that means the same as <u>anger</u>.

_____

1

7. Who trips Eloise? How do you know?

_____

_____

1

8. What do you think is most likely to happen next in the story?

Tick **one**.

Thandie moves to a new school. ☐

Nicola and Thandie become friends. ☐

Jamal tells their teacher about Eloise's bullying. ☐

Eloise decides to be nice to Thandie. ☐

1

Well done! END OF READING TEST 1!

Should zoos be banned?

Aisha and Josh both love the natural world. However, they disagree about whether animals should be kept in zoos. Here's what they think.

Aisha

I know that zoos aren't the best place for wild animals. Animals should always live in their own natural habitats if possible. But it's not that simple. There are some species that are very rare and endangered. If we didn't look after the last northern white rhinos in a zoo, they wouldn't exist at all.

Good zoos don't snatch animals from the wild for our entertainment. Modern zoos look after endangered species. They can be places for rescued animals that are too young or vulnerable to be released back into the wild. They provide a safe environment for breeding programmes. They also give you a chance to see the animals for yourself. Most people can't go on safari. Sure, TV nature programmes are interesting. However, seeing a living, breathing creature gives you a sense of wonder about nature. This is so important for educating people. Otherwise, some species might become extinct.

Lastly, all this work needs to be paid for. Without the money visitors pay, zoos couldn't look after the animals, do research and carry out breeding programmes to save endangered species.

Josh

Zoos are a really old-fashioned idea. It's so horrible seeing amazing animals shut in cages. They pace up and down. They're bored and frustrated. It must be so lonely and depressing. I don't understand how anyone can enjoy seeing such magnificent creatures locked up. Animals don't exist just for our entertainment!

Even worse, you can't even get close to the animals. They're always behind a fence or some glass. You can see them much better on TV nature programmes. The environments that the zoos create are nothing like the animals' real

homes. Some of them are badly designed and managed. The zoo owners don't take animal welfare seriously. Some zoos are just money-making businesses.

Zoos aren't even good at saving endangered animals. The only way to stop species becoming extinct is to change how we humans behave. We must protect natural habitats and give animals the space to live freely.

People used to watch live animals doing tricks at circuses. Nowadays, lots of countries have banned this because people realise that it's cruel. One day, people will think the same about zoos.

Marks

1. Who thinks it's ok to keep animals in zoos?

_____

_____

1

2. Which animal does Aisha claim would be extinct if it wasn't kept in a zoo?

_____

1

10 MINS

Marks

3. Rescued animals are described as being *too young or vulnerable to be released back into the wild.*

Circle the word below that means the same as <u>vulnerable</u> in this sentence.

old   sick   safe   defenceless

1

4. Josh and Aisha disagree about TV nature programmes. Explain how their opinions are different.

_____

_____

_____

_____

_____

_____

_____

2

5. Look at the paragraph beginning: *Even worse, you can't even get close to animals.*

Find and **copy** a word that means the same as <u>health and happiness</u>.

_____

KEEP IT GOING!

1

26

10 MINS

6. Where does Josh say people used to go to see live animals?

_____

_____

Marks

1

7. Josh calls animals kept in zoos *magnificent creatures* and *amazing animals*. What effect do these phrases have on the reader?

_____

_____

1

8. Tick **true** or **false** for each statement about Josh and Aisha.

	True	False
Aisha says zoos look after endangered species.		
Aisha thinks it's horrible to see animals in cages.		
Josh says people shouldn't have to pay to go to zoos.		
Josh thinks zoos are old-fashioned.		

2

Well done! END OF READING TEST 2!

The Fox and the Grapes

A fable by Aesop

Grapes are growing, round and ripe,
High upon the vine.
Fox says, as he licks his lips,
"Those grapes will soon by mine."

The grapes look plump and juicy.
The fox, on his hind legs,
Stretches up to reach for them
Just like a dog that begs.

Fox jumps and keeps on jumping
To try and take his treat.
The grapes will be so tasty:
Succulent and sweet.

At last, the hungry fox gives up.
He's tried for many an hour.
He cannot reach the fruit and cries:
"I bet those grapes are sour."

MORAL
If something is good,
But it's not to be had,
Don't fool yourself
By pretending it's bad.

Celia Warren

Marks

1. What is the name of the plant that produces grapes?

_____

_____

1

2. Look at the first two verses.

a. Find and **copy** four words that tell you what the grapes look like.

1. _____

2. _____

3. _____

4. _____

1

b. What does the fox look like when it stretches to reach the grapes?

_____

_____

1

3. Look at this line: *The fox, on his hind legs*

What does the word <u>hind</u> mean?

_____

1

Marks

4. In the fourth verse, the fox says: *I bet those grapes are sour.*

Why does the fox say this?

_____

_____

_____

_____

_____

2

5. This poem ends with the <u>MORAL</u>. Which of these statements best describes what a moral is?

Tick **one**.

the final verse or paragraph of a poem or story ☐

the lesson that you can learn from a poem or story ☐

the most exciting part of the plot ☐

the description of whether characters are good or bad ☐

1

KEEP IT GOING!

Marks

6. What do you think the moral of this poem is? Explain in your own words.

_____

_____

_____

_____

_____

2

7. This poem is described as a fable. Which of these statements best describes what a fable is?

Tick **one**.

a traditional story involving supernatural creatures or events ☐

a story from the past that many people believe might be true ☐

a short tale with an animal character that teaches a moral lesson ☐

a rhyming poem about an animal character and some food ☐

1

Well done! END OF READING TEST 3!

Marks

1.   33 + 33 =

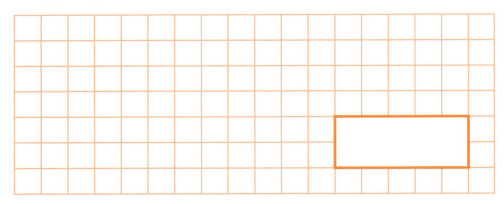

1

2.   ☐ × 4 = 36

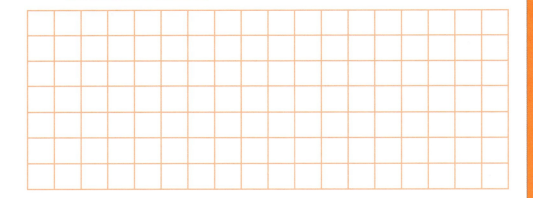

1

KEEP IT GOING!

3. 100 + 100 + 50 =

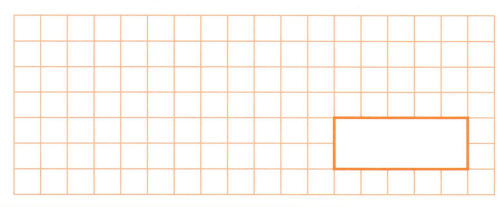

1

4. 1010 − 999 =

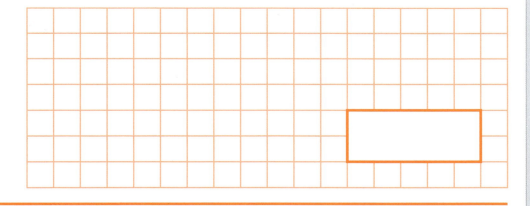

1

5. $\frac{3}{7} + \frac{2}{7} =$

1

6. $21 \times 5 =$

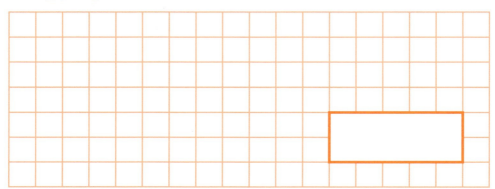

Marks

1

7. $830 - 475 =$

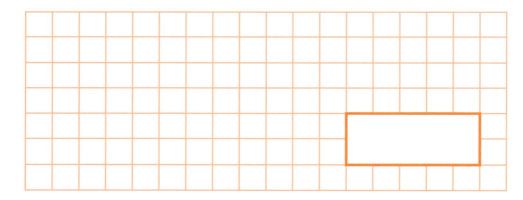

1

8. $2 - 4 =$

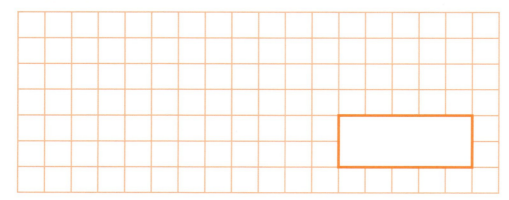

1

10 MINS

9.   1627 + 4355 =

Marks

1

10.

Show your method

   6 | 7   9   2

2

Well done! END OF MATHS SET A TEST 1!

Maths

Set A Test 2: Reasoning

10 MINS

Marks

1. Shade $\frac{1}{3}$ of each set of shapes.

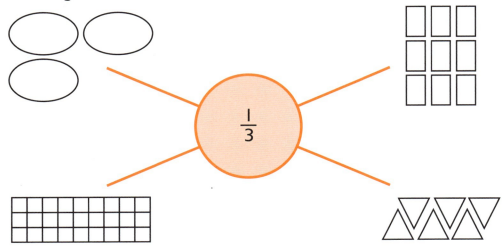

1

2. Write the missing digits to complete this addition.

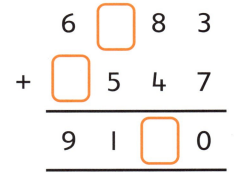

1

Marks

3.

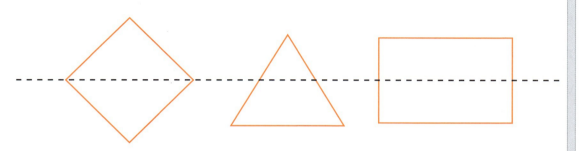

Tim draws a straight line through three shapes. He wants it to be a line of symmetry for each shape.

Explain the mistake Tim has made.

_____

_____

1

4. Round 7445 to the nearest 10, then round the answer to the nearest 100 and then to the nearest 1000.

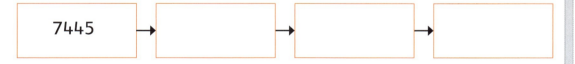

7445 → ☐ → ☐ → ☐

1

Marks

5. There are 21 staff and 200 children in a school.

$\frac{2}{7}$ of the staff walk to school and $\frac{3}{5}$ of the children walk to school.

How many people walk to school altogether?

Show your method

people

2

---

6. Prisha's family go to the cinema.

The three children's tickets cost £23.40 altogether and the two adult's tickets cost £22.60 altogether.

Her parents have £50 to spend on the night out. How much do they have left over for popcorn?

SCREEN 1

Show your method

£

2

7. The bar chart shows the amount of waste collected by a recycling van six days a week.

Marks

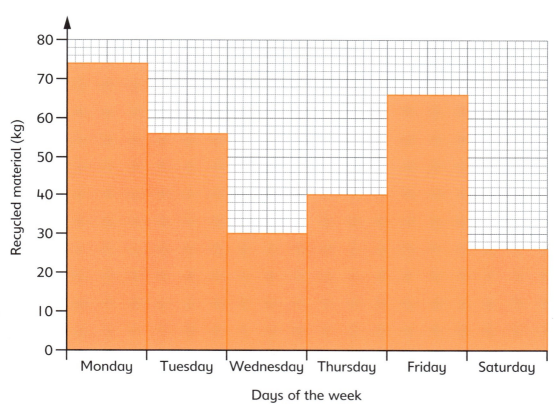

a. Complete this sentence:

On _____ there was 10kg more waste collected than

on _____, but 16kg less than on _____.

1

b. How much more waste was collected on the busiest day than the quietest day?

_____ kg

1

Well done! END OF MATHS SET A TEST 2!

Marks

1. Alexandra takes four digit cards.

| 3 | 7 | 2 | 5 |

She arranges the four cards twice: to make the largest and the smallest possible numbers.

Write, **in words**, the two numbers she makes.

_____

_____

_____

_____

1

2. Draw lines to match each fraction to its decimal equivalent.

| $\frac{1}{4}$ | $\frac{1}{100}$ | $\frac{1}{10}$ | $\frac{1}{2}$ |

| 0.5 | 0.25 | 0.1 | 0.01 |

1

3. Noah draws two axes and starts to plot a square. He wants each side of the square to be 3 units long. Plot the remaining corners and draw the square. Write the coordinates next to each corner.

Marks

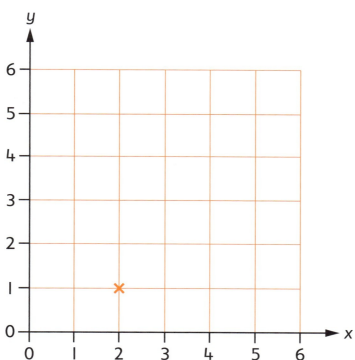

1

4. Write numbers in the spaces to complete these calculations:

$$2 \times \boxed{} \times 5 = 70$$

$$5 \times \boxed{} \times 4 = 60$$

$$5 \times \boxed{} \times 5 = 50$$

1

Marks

5. The **24-hour digital clock** below is fast.

a. How many **seconds** fast is it?

seconds

1

b. Show what time will appear on each clock at twenty past seven in the evening.

1

6. A grocer buys coconuts in packs of 6. He then sells single coconuts for £2 each. The shopkeeper makes £84 from selling coconuts. How many packs did he use?

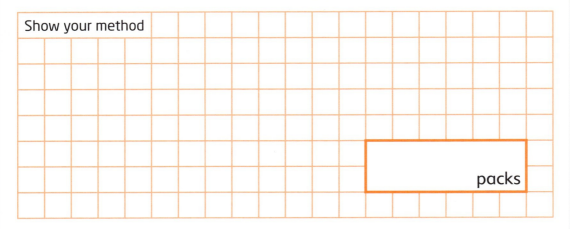

Show your method

packs

2

Well done! END OF MATHS SET A TEST 3!

Maths

Set B Test 1: Arithmetic

10 MINS

Marks

1. $\frac{1}{2}$ of 20 =

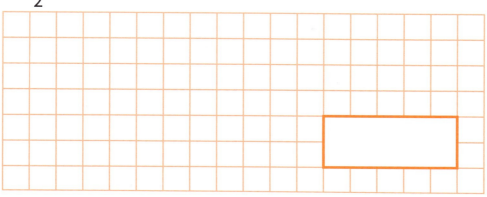

1

2.   6350 − 1000 =

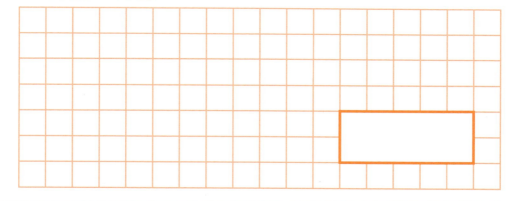

1

3. $\frac{1}{100} + \frac{1}{100} + \frac{1}{100} =$

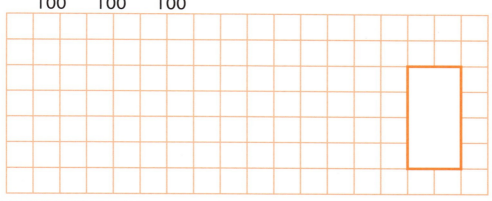

1

Marks

4.   3 × 3 × 2 =

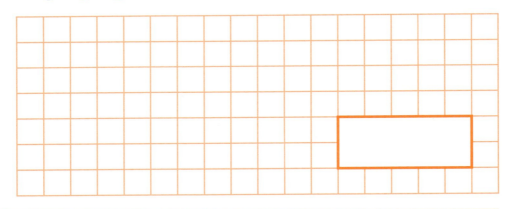

1

5.   72 ÷ 8 =

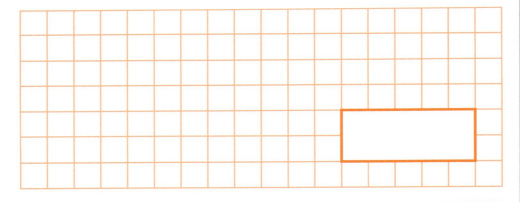

1

6.   1200 + 401 =

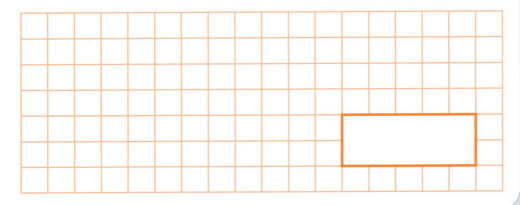

1

Marks

7.   274 + 535 =

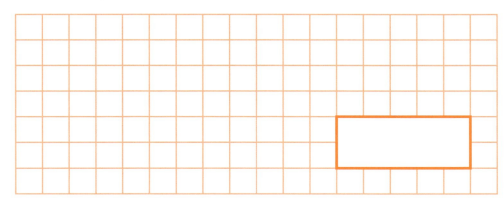

1

8.   43 ÷ 10 =

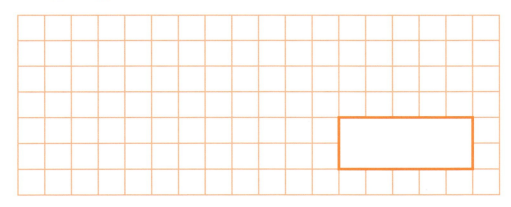

1

10 MINS

Marks

9. 4306 − 2436 =

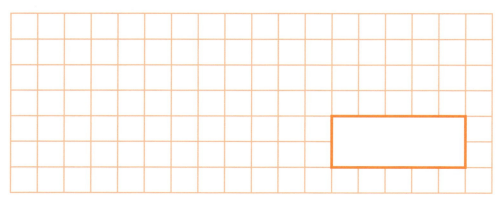

1

10. 54 × 7 =

Show your method

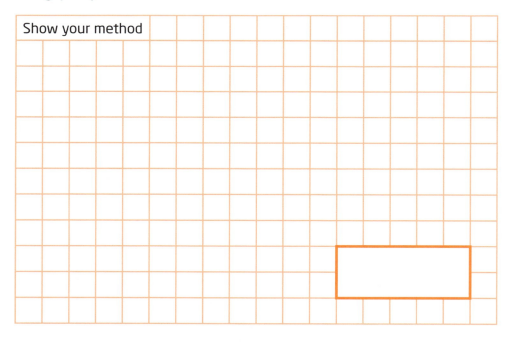

2

Well done! END OF MATHS SET B TEST 1!

Maths
Set B Test 2: Reasoning

10 MINS

Marks

1. Sanjay uses this chart to practise making Roman numbers.

I	V	X	L	C
one	five	ten	fifty	one hundred

Circle all the correct numbers. One has been done for you.

(4 = IV)   14 = XIIII   24 = XXIV   37 = XXXIV

55 = LV   69 = LXIX   85 = LXXV   90 = XC

1

2. Write the missing digits to make this division correct.

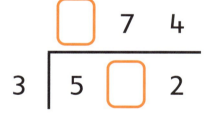

1

3. Using numerals, write these numbers in order from **smallest to largest**.

Two thousand, six hundred and seventy-one

One thousand, five hundred and ninety-nine

One thousand, one hundred and eighty

Two thousand and forty-seven

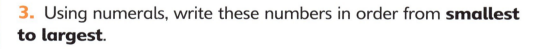

1

Marks

4. Joanne draws a diagram showing the distances between three cities: A, B and C.

A   B   C

634km   287km

Estimate the total distance from A to C, to the nearest 10km

km

1

---

5. Point C is translated to D.

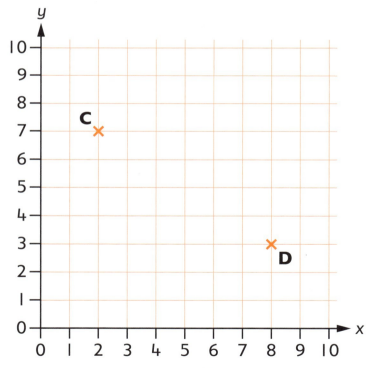

Tick the box next to the correct translation:

(6,4) ☐   (−6,−4) ☐   (6,−4) ☐   (−6,4) ☐

1

6. Zoe draws a shape on the playground. She then measures each side in cm. Calculate the perimeter of the shape, giving your answer in **metres**.

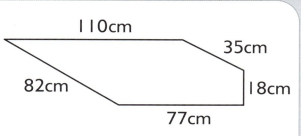

110cm

35cm

82cm

18cm

77cm

Marks

Show your method

m

2

7. A school has raised £50 for charity. They have a vote to decide on the most popular charities.

They give half of all the money to the most popular charity. Half of the remaining money goes to the second most popular charity. The rest is split equally between the third and fourth most popular charities. Complete the chart to show how much each charity receives.

Popularity	Charity	Amount given
1	Cats and dogs home	
2	Help the elderly	
3	Help the homeless	
4	Donkey sanctuary	

1

Well done! END OF MATHS SET B TEST 2!

10 MINS

Marks

1. Draw lines to place each decimal in the correct position on the number line. 0.25 has been done for you.

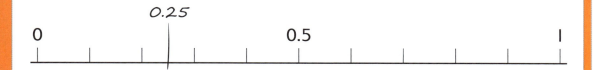

0.25   0.9   0.45   0.68   0.07

1

2. These symbols each have a numeric value.

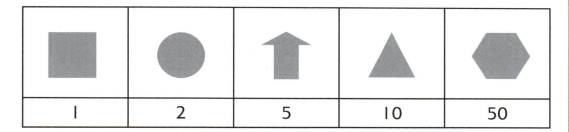

■	●	⬆	▲	⬡
1	2	5	10	50

 = 13

Write the value for these sets of symbols:

1

50

Marks

3. Katie says, 'I can do 84 × 3 in my head, no problem!'
Use Katie's method to multiply 234 × 4.

$80 \times 3 + 4 \times 3$
$240 + 12 = 252$

_____

_____

_____

_____

_____

1

4. a. Jamie draws a straight line through a square.
He puts an x in one of the right-angles.

Identify all the angles inside the square.
Put an 'x' in each right-angle, a 'y' in each acute angle, and a 'z' in
each obtuse angle.

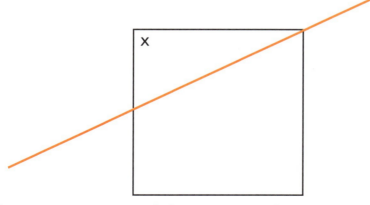

x

1

b. Write the correct names of the two new shapes
that Jamie has made.

_____ and _____

1

51

5. Tina checks how much money is in her money box each week. She plots the amounts on a graph.

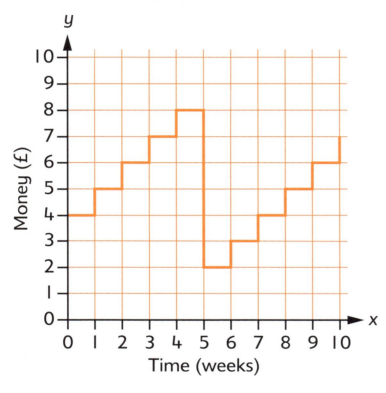

Time (weeks)

Explain what has happened to make the graph look like this.

_____

_____

_____

_____

_____

_____

_____

Marks

1

6. Joe has a 500g bag of seeds to fill the school's four bird-feeders.

The first feeder takes 140g of the seeds.
The second feeder takes 180g of the seeds.
The third feeder takes 120g of the seeds.

Joe then goes to the school caretaker who gives him another 250g of seeds.

Finally, Joe puts 210g of seeds into the last feeder.
How many grams of seeds will Joe have left over?

Marks

Show your method

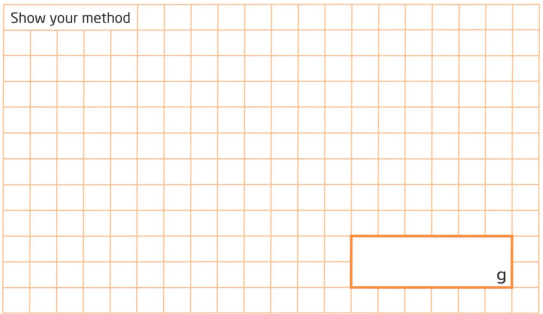

g

2

Well done! END OF MATHS SET B TEST 3!

53

Answers

Q	Mark scheme for Grammar and Punctuation Test 1	Marks
1	**Award 1 mark** if 'book' and 'shelf' are underlined. **Grammar essentials:** A noun is a naming word for a person, place, thing, animal, idea or concept.	1
2	**Award 1 mark** if 'What a brilliant idea that is!' is ticked. **Grammar and punctuation essentials:** The second sentence is an exclamation and is punctuated correctly as it starts with 'What', contains a verb and ends with an exclamation mark. The first sentence is a question (which should end in a question mark, not an exclamation mark), the third sentence is a statement (which should end in a full stop, not a question mark) and the fourth sentence is an exclamation (which should end in an exclamation mark, not a question mark).	1
3	**Award 1 mark** for all three prefixes matched correctly as follows: 'impossible', 'unavailable', 'disagree'. **Grammar essentials:** A prefix is a string of letters added to the beginning of a word to turn it into another word. It does not alter the spelling of the word it is joined to.	1
4	**Award 1 mark** for each row correctly ticked in this following order: subordinate clause, main clause, subordinate clause. **Grammar essentials:** A subordinate clause is introduced by a subordinating conjunction. It is dependent on a main clause – it doesn't make sense on its own.	1
5	**Award 1 mark** for: 'My dog likes going for walks**,** fetching sticks**,** swimming and chasing rabbits.' **Punctuation essentials:** Commas can be used to separate items in a list (but not before 'and').	1
6	**Award 1 mark** for 'madly', 'specially' and 'angrily' spelled correctly. **Grammar essentials:** A suffix is a letter or string of letters added to the end of a word to turn it into another word. When adding a suffix to a word ending in y with a consonant before it, the y is changed to i. However, the y is kept when adding the suffix ing, e.g. cry - crying.	1
7	**Award 1 mark** for correctly matching as follows: we had – we'd, we are – we're, we have – we've. **Punctuation essentials:** An apostrophe can be used to indicate a missing letter or letters (contraction).	1
8	**Award 1 mark** for 'it' written in the box. **Grammar essentials:** A pronoun can be used to replace a noun, noun phrase or proper noun. It aids cohesion and avoids repetition.	1
9	**Award 1 mark** for the following words circled: we, london, buckingham, palace. **Punctuation essentials:** A sentence starts with a capital letter. Proper nouns also start with a capital letter. Proper nouns include the names of towns ('London') and places ('Buckingham Palace').	1
10	**Award 1 mark** if 'had finished' has been ticked. **Grammar essentials:** This sentence requires the past perfect verb form to indicate an action that occurred before another action in the past.	1
11	**Award 1 mark** if 'mine' has been circled. **Grammar essentials:** A possessive pronoun replaces a person or thing that belongs to someone or something.	1
12	**Award 1 mark** if 'What an amazing book that was' has been ticked. **Grammar and punctuation essentials:** An exclamation sentence starts with 'How' or 'What', contains a verb and ends with an exclamation mark.	1
	Total	12

Q	Mark scheme for Grammar and Punctuation Test 2	Marks
1	**Award 1 mark** if 'quietly' has been underlined. **Grammar essentials:** An adverb can tell you more about a verb. It can say how something happens. Remember, not all adverbs end in 'ly' and not all words ending in 'ly' are adverbs!	1
2	**Award 1 mark** if 'I have two sisters and one brother.' has been ticked. **Grammar essentials:** A statement is a sentence that tells you something.	1

Q	Mark scheme for Grammar and Punctuation Test 2 continued	Marks
3	**Award 1 mark** if all three have been correctly matched as follows: 'unhelpful', 'disappear', 'misspell'. **Grammar essentials:** A prefix is a string of letters added to the beginning of a word to turn it into another word. It does not alter the spelling of the word it is joined to.	1
4	**Award 1 mark** if both 'a' and 'the' have been circled. **Grammar essentials:** A determiner indicates whether a noun is specific/known (e.g. 'the') or more general/un-known (e.g. 'a/an').	1
5	**Award 1 mark** for 'Mia **and** Ed really enjoyed the film **but** Ushma found it boring.' **Grammar essentials:** A co-ordinating conjunction can join two words or phrases of equal importance.	1
6	**Award 1 mark** if 'were watching' has been ticked. **Grammar essentials:** This sentence requires the use of the past progressive tense which describes a continuous action that took place in the past.	1
7	**Award 1 mark** if 'preposition' has been ticked. **Grammar essentials:** A preposition links a noun, pronoun or noun phrase to another word in the sentence.	1
8	**Award 1 mark** for: "Let's decide what to buy Mum for her birthday," Martha said to Dad. **Punctuation essentials:** In direct speech, inverted commas come at the start of the opening speech and after the final punctuation of the speech.	1
9	**Award 1 mark** for: 'boxes', 'classes' and 'children', spelled correctly. **Grammar essentials:** To make most nouns plural, simply add the suffix 's' or 'es'. Some nouns have an irregular plural form, e.g. children, men, mice.	1
10	**a. Award 1 mark** if 'It's' is circled in the first sentence. **b. Award 1 mark** if 'Faye's' is circled in the second sentence. **Punctuation essentials:** An apostrophe can be used to show ownership (possession) or to indicate a missing letter or letters (contraction).	1 1
11	**Award 1 mark** for each row ticked correctly in the following order: subordinate clause, main clause, main clause. **Grammar essentials:** A subordinate clause is introduced by a subordinating conjunction. It is dependent on a main clause – it doesn't make sense on its own.	1
	Total	12

Q	Mark scheme for Grammar and Punctuation Test 3	Marks
1	**Award 1 mark** if 'enormous' has been underlined. **Grammar essentials:** An adjective can come before the noun, as here, to modify it, or after the verb 'to be' as its complement.	1
2	**Award 1 mark** if 'Wash your hands before eating' has been ticked. **Grammar essentials:** A command is a sentence that tells you to do something. It usually ends with a full stop but may end with an exclamation mark.	1
3	**Award 1 mark** for: 'Grace's books turned up in the lost property box.' **Punctuation essentials:** An apostrophe can be used to indicate ownership (possession).	1
4	**Award 1 mark** for 'because', 'since' or 'as'. **Grammar essentials:** A subordinating conjunction introduces a subordinate clause.	1
5	**Award 1 mark** for: 'regularly', 'happily' and 'finally', correctly spelled. **Grammar essentials:** A suffix is a letter or string of letters added to the end of a word to turn it into another word. When adding a suffix to a word ending with y with a consonant before it, they y is changed to i. However, they y is kept when adding the suffix ing, e.g. cry - crying.	1

Q	Mark scheme for Grammar and Punctuation Test 3 continued	Marks
6	**Award I mark** if 'Mum's always saying we need peace and quiet.' has been ticked. **Grammar essentials:** In Standard English, correct grammar is used.	I
7	**Award I mark** for the commas placed correctly: 'Dougie gave me a hat**,** a pair of slippers**,** a scarf and some socks for my birthday.' **Punctuation essentials:** Commas can be used to separate items in a list (but not before 'and').	I
8	**Award I mark** if 'After our picnic, we lay in the sun and dozed.' has been ticked. **Grammar and punctuation essentials:** When a sentence starts with an adverbial (fronted adverbial), it is followed by a comma.	I
9	**Award I mark** if 'We are performing a gymnastics routine for our parents.' has been ticked. **Grammar essentials:** This sentence uses the present progressive tense of the verb 'perform' to show a continuous action in the present.	I
10	**Award I mark** if 'hers' has been circled. **Grammar essentials:** A possessive pronoun replaces a person or thing that belongs to someone or something.	I
11	**Award I mark** for each row correctly ticked as follows: present tense, past tense, past tense. **Grammar essentials:** The present tense is used for an action that takes place in the present. The past tense is used for an action that took place in the past.	I
12	**Award I mark** if 'What an amazing time we had at the cinema' has been ticked. **Grammar and punctuation essentials:** An exclamation sentence starts with 'How' or 'What', contains a verb and ends with an exclamation mark.	I
	Total	12

Q	Mark scheme for Reading Test I: The Trip	Marks
I	**Award I mark** for: eagerly	I
2	**Award I mark** for answers referring Eloise's dominance over the other children. For example: We know because she is 'issuing orders' to the others.	I
3	**Award 2 marks** for answers referring to how her short time at school seems longer because of the bullying. For example: Thandie has only been at school two weeks, but it feels much longer because she is being bullied every day. **Award I mark** for answers that refer to bullying but not the short time she has spent at school. For example: Because she is being bullied all the time.	2
4	**a. Award I mark** for: tag **b. Award I mark** for: Jamal, Henry and Nicola OR Jamal and Henry.	I I
5	**Award I mark** for answers referring to checking that no one was watching. For example: She wants to make sure the teacher isn't watching.	I
6	**Award I mark** for: outrage	I
7	**Award I mark** for naming Nicola and giving a reason such as: • We know because she winks at Thandie. • We know it can't have been Jamal or Henry because they are 'dumbfounded', so it can only have been Nicola.	I
8	**Award I mark** for: Nicola and Thandie become friends.	I
	Total	10

Q	Mark scheme for Reading Test 2: Should zoos be banned?	Marks
I	**Award I mark** for: Aisha	I
2	**Award I mark** for: northern white rhinos	I
3	**Award I mark** for: defenceless	I

Q	Mark scheme for Reading Test 2: Should zoos be banned? continued	Marks
4	**Award 2 marks** for answers referring to how Aisha thinks TV programmes are not as good as seeing the animals for real and Josh thinks you can see the animals better. For example: Josh thinks you can see the animals better on the TV, but Aisha thinks TV is not as good as seeing them in real life. **Award 1 mark** for answers explaining only Aisha's or Josh's opinions.	2
5	**Award 1 mark** for: welfare	1
6	**Award 1 mark** for: (at) circuses	1
7	**Award 1 mark** for answers referring to sympathy for the animals. For example: It makes you feel sorry for the animals because they shouldn't be locked up.	1
8	**Award 2 marks** for four correct answers. **Award 1 mark** for two or three correct answers. *(see table below)*	2

	True	False
Aisha says zoos look after endangered species.	✔	
Aisha thinks it's horrible to see animals in cages.		✔
Josh says people shouldn't have to pay to go to zoos.		✔
Josh thinks zoos are old-fashioned.	✔	

	Total	**10**

Q	Mark scheme for Reading Test 3: The Fox and the Grapes	Marks
1	**Award 1 mark** for: vine	1
2	**a. Award 1 mark** for all of the following: round, ripe, plump, juicy **b. Award 1 mark** for: a dog that begs	1 1
3	**Award 1 mark** for: back, or rear	1
4	**Award 2 marks** for answers referring to how the fox cannot reach the grapes and how he is pretending he doesn't want them anymore. For example: The fox can't reach the grapes because they're too high, so he pretends he doesn't want them because they're sour. **Award 1 mark** for answers referring only to how the fox cannot reach the grapes or how he is pretending he doesn't want them.	2
5	**Award 1 mark** for: the lesson that you can learn from a poem or story	1
6	**Award 2 marks** for answers that refer to the idea of 'sour grapes'. For example: The moral is that you shouldn't pretend something is rubbish just because you can't have it. **Award 1 mark** for answers referring to how you can't always get what you want but without reference to the pretending. OR **Award 1 mark** for answers referring to pretending something is bad but without reference to how it's not available.	2
7	**Award 1 mark** for: a short tale with animal characters that teaches a moral lesson.	1

	Total	**10**

Q	Mark scheme for Maths Set A Test 1: Arithmetic	Marks
1	66	1
2	9	1
3	250	1
4	11	1
5	$\frac{5}{7}$	1
6	105	1
7	355	1

Q	Mark scheme for Maths Set A Test 1: Arithmetic continued	Marks
8	−2	1
9	5982	1
10	132 **Award 1 mark** for a correct method but one arithmetical error.	2
	Total	11

Q	Mark scheme for Maths Set A Test 2: Reasoning	Marks
1	Shading of: any one of the three ovals; any three of the rectangles, any two of the triangles and any nine of the squares.	1
2	$$\begin{array}{r} 6\ \mathbf{5}\ 8\ 3 \\ +\ \mathbf{2}\ 5\ 4\ 7 \\ \hline 9\ 1\ \mathbf{3}\ 0 \\ \hline \end{array}$$	1
3	The explanation should make it clear that the triangle is not arranged symmetrically. Children might say that it is not the same shape on either side of the dotted line, or that it needs to be turned or rotated to get a line of symmetry in line with the other shapes.	1
4	7445 ⟶ 7450 ⟶ 7500 ⟶ 8000	1
5	6 staff + 120 children = 126 people **Award 1 mark** for the correct approach but with a maximum of one arithmetical error.	2
6	£4 left over **Award 1 mark** for demonstration of the correct approach but with one arithmetical error.	2
7	**a.** On **Thursday** there was 10kg more waste collected than on **Wednesday** but 16kg less than on **Tuesday**. **b.** 48kg	1 1
	Total	10

Q	Mark scheme for Maths Set A Test 3: Reasoning	Marks
1	Seven thousand, five hundred and thirty-two Two thousand, three hundred and fifty-seven Spelling does not have to be exact, but both numbers must be correct to award the mark.	1
2	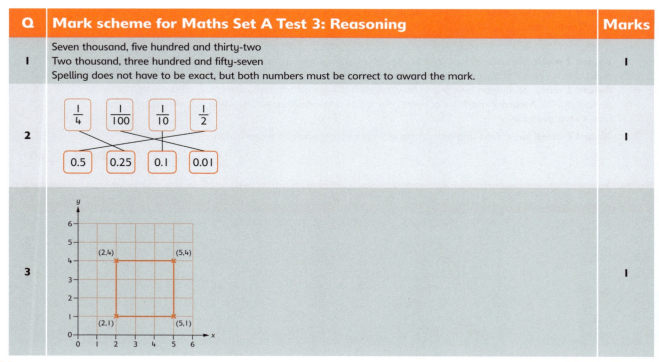	1
3		1

Q	Mark scheme for Maths Set A Test 3: Reasoning continued	Marks
4	$2 \times \mathbf{7} \times 5 = 70$ $5 \times \mathbf{3} \times 4 = 60$ $5 \times \mathbf{2} \times 5 = 50$	1
5	**a.** $3 \times 60 = 180$ seconds **b.** 	1 1
6	7 packs of coconuts **Award I mark** for demonstration of the correct approach but with one arithmetical error.	2
	Total	**8**

Q	Mark scheme for Maths Set B Test 1: Arithmetic	Marks
1	10	1
2	5350	1
3	$\frac{3}{100}$	1
4	18	1
5	9	1
6	1601	1
7	809	1
8	4.3	1
9	1870	1
10	378 **Award I mark** for correct approach to solving the answer, but with a maximum of one arithmetical error.	2
	Total	**11**

Q	Mark scheme for Maths Set B Test 2: Reasoning	Marks
1	(4 = IV) 14 = XIIII (24 = XXIV) 37 = XXXIV (55 = LV) (69 = LXIX) 85 = LXXV (90 = XC) All correct to award mark	1
2	$\begin{array}{r} 1\,7\,4 \\ 3\,\overline{\smash{)}\,5\,2\,2} \end{array}$	1
3	1180 1599 2047 2671	1
4	920km	1
5	(6, −4) is correct	1
6	3.22m **Award I mark** for a correct approach to completing the calculation but with one arithmetical error.	2

59

Q	Mark scheme for Maths Set B Test 2: Reasoning continued	Marks
7	<table><tr><th>Popularity</th><th>Charity</th><th>Amount given</th></tr><tr><td>1</td><td>Cats and dogs home</td><td>£25</td></tr><tr><td>2</td><td>Help the elderly</td><td>£12.50</td></tr><tr><td>3</td><td>Help the homeless</td><td>£6.25</td></tr><tr><td>4</td><td>Donkey sanctuary</td><td>£6.25</td></tr></table>	1
	Total	**8**

Q	Mark scheme for Maths Set B Test 3: Reasoning	Marks
1	**Award 1 mark** if all numbers are reasonably accurate, with no ambiguity of children's intentions. 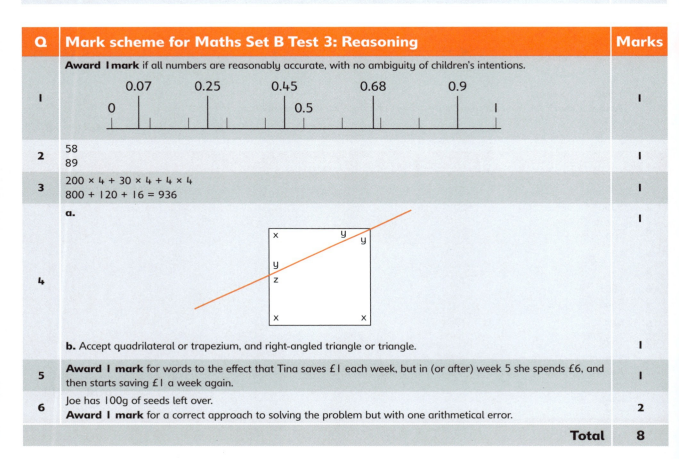	1
2	58 89	1
3	$200 \times 4 + 30 \times 4 + 4 \times 4$ $800 + 120 + 16 = 936$	1
4	**a.**	1
	b. Accept quadrilateral or trapezium, and right-angled triangle or triangle.	1
5	**Award 1 mark** for words to the effect that Tina saves £1 each week, but in (or after) week 5 she spends £6, and then starts saving £1 a week again.	1
6	Joe has 100g of seeds left over. **Award 1 mark** for a correct approach to solving the problem but with one arithmetical error.	2
	Total	**8**

How to administer the spelling tests

10 MINS

There are three short spelling tests in this book with four questions in each test. Grammar and Punctuation Test 1 and Spelling Test 1 make up one full test which should take ten minutes in total to complete.

However, you should allow your child as much time as they need.

Read the instructions in the box below.

> *Listen carefully to the instructions I am going to give you.*
>
> *I am going to read four sentences to you. Each sentence on your answer sheet has a missing word. Listen carefully to the missing word and write it in the space provided, making sure you spell the word correctly.*
>
> *I will read the word, then the word within the sentence, then repeat the word a third time.*
>
> *Do you have any questions?*

Read the spellings as follows:

- Give the question number, 'Spelling 1'
- Say, 'The word is...'
- Read the whole sentence to show the word in context
- Repeat, 'The word is...'

Leave at least a 12-second gap between each spelling.

At the end re-read all four questions. Then say, 'This is the end of the test. Please put down your pencil or pen.'

Each correct answer should be awarded **1 mark**.

Spelling test transcripts

Spelling Test 1

Spelling 1: The word is **crying**. Beth started **crying** when she cut her finger. The word is **crying**.

Spelling 2: The word is **ground**. The **ground** was frozen after a frosty night. The word is **ground**.

Spelling 3: The word is **witch**. I dressed up as a **witch** for Halloween. The word is **witch**.

Spelling 4: The word is **disobeys**. Our puppy always **disobeys** us. The word is **disobeys**.

Spelling Test 2

Spelling 1: The word is **science**. We are learning about evaporation in **science**. The word is **science**.

Spelling 2: The word is **where**. I showed Mum **where** she had left her bag. The word is **where**.

Spelling 3: The word is **condition**. The football pitch was in a poor **condition**. The word is **condition**.

Spelling 4: The word is **technique**. Jon had a good **technique** for learning his tables. The word is **technique**.

Spelling Test 3

Spelling 1: The word is **weighed**. I **weighed** the sugar and flour, then added the butter. The word is **weighed**.

Spelling 2: The word is **echo**. We heard an **echo** at the back of the cave. The word is **echo**.

Spelling 3: The word is **musician**. The **musician** bowed as the audience clapped. The word is **musician**.

Spelling 4: The word is **except**. Everyone **except** Bhavini could dive off the board. The word is **except**.

Progress chart

Fill in your score in the table below to see how well you've done.

10 MINS

Test number	Score	Percentage		Percentage	
Grammar, Punctuation and Spelling Test 1	/12			0–33%	Good try! You need more practice in some topics – ask an adult to help you.
Grammar, Punctuation and Spelling Test 2	/12				
Grammar, Punctuation and Spelling Test 3	/12			34–69%	You're doing really well. Ask for extra help for any topics you found tricky.
Reading Test 1	/10				
Reading Test 2	/10			70–100%	You're a 10-Minute SATs Test star – good work!
Reading Test 3	/10				
Maths Set A: Test 1					
Maths Set A: Test 2	/29				
Maths Set A: Test 3					
Maths Set B: Test 1					
Maths Set B: Test 2	/27				
Maths Set B: Test 3					

Reward Certificate

Well done!

You have completed all of the 10-Minute Tests

Name: _____   Date: _____

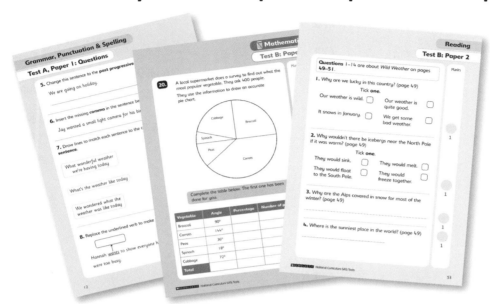

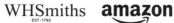